DEDICATION

This book is lovingly dedicated to my Irish mother-in-law, the "Mom" who is responsible for bits of the content. She also helped raise my seven children and lived with a laugh on her lips till she was ninety-six years old.

...AND IN CONCLUSION

What life has to offer after ninety years.

By Mary S. Shern (Who should know)

Illustrated by Alan Low

Table of Contents

...AND IN CONCLUSION

Introduction

This little book is all about being OLD. There isn't any doubt about this. The fact is that the number of people who qualify for that adjective is growing at a scary rate. It's no secret that some folks are wondering how fewer and fewer people are going to provide for more and more senior citizens – or even wondering why they should? Please don't expect my book to provide you with all the answers. It is simply a motley collection of personal, borrowed, and brashly stolen thoughts - sometimes heartfelt and occasionally irreverent – about how it feels to be in the final phase of one's earthly existence.

The author is highly qualified, having been around for more than ninety years, and having experienced the prescribed quota of triumphs and tragedies. A few years ago I moved into a senior retirement facility where I share my daily existence with about two hundred other old souls, most of whom recall the Great Depression and have saved immense quantities of string and tinfoil. They still feel guilty when they cannot clean their plates at dinner. Many of us not only recall but also served in World War II. We cry at parades and retain a hearty, patriotic respect for our men and women in uniform.

It would be extremely foolish to contend that growing old is all fun and games. We often see a line-up of canes, walkers and wheel chairs. We are menaced now and then by reckless drivers in motorized scooters. We run into a few crotchety old characters who are so hard to please that one sometimes wonders if they came out of the womb, complaining! On the other hand, many of us still find our life to be very satisfactory indeed – as long as it provides a generous serving of laughs, good company, tasty food and fine wine. Generally speaking, it does.

For senior citizens, reading this book may provide no more than a pleasant peek into familiar territory. If we have any serious purpose in mind,

it, would be a faint hope that there might be some improvement in inter-generational understanding and communication. The pace of change in today's society causes us to wonder if we're all speaking the same language.

We do realize that the young may be too busy sending and receiving amazing text messages to read our book.

However, those who hope to inherit Grandfather's estate might find a few helpful hints. We know your grandfather and lately he is considering leaving his money to a Society for the Prevention of Cruelty to Brain-injured Greyhounds.

CHAPTER 1

"When Forever is Much Shorter than Before"

One of the grandkids posed this not-too-tactful question: "Gram, when did you start being an old person?" The title to this chapter, taken from a lyric in the movie "Gigi", is probably about as close as we could get to an answer. I asked a stranger on an elevator one day if he knew where the summer had gone. He replied quite solemnly that he had asked his family that question that very morning. "And," he went on, "they didn't have a clue." The truth is, we don't know where last month went, or last year or even all the years before that. Old age is not a happening. It creeps up on us, while clocks are ticking and old Father Time is doing his dastardly deeds; until at last it becomes evident that the curtain has gone up on our final act.

Clearly, most of those who have not yet arrived at the old age stage of life, or who don't think they have, are not looking forward to it. Small wonder we should feel that way when we read how our wise ancestors described it:

> *"... old age is a regret."*   *Disraeli*
> *"... our play's last act."*   *Cicero*
> *"...a period...closest to the end"*   *Hakewill*
> *"...a woman's hell"*   *de L'endes*
> *"...an island surrounded by death"*   *Montalvo*
> *"...an incurable disease"*   *Seneca*

It really shouldn't surprise us to know that many people look upon old age as being synonymous with pain, wrinkles, disabilities, incontinence, illness, dementia and imminent death. On the other hand, before throwing our readers into a state of clinical depression we hasten to point out that there are some other points of view. The great poet, Robert Browning, in a work titled Rabbi Ben Ezra, wrote:

> *"Grow old along with me*
> *The best is yet to be*
> *The last of life, for which*
> *The first was made."*

No matter what our opinion might be, even face lifts and Botox haven't changed the unassailable fact that we're all growing older as we read these words. You might passionately wish to resist that relentless march, but it doesn't take a barrel of smarts to see that the only way to avoid it is to die young. This is, of course, NOT an alternative people in general are happy to embrace. However, when an individual can recognize and accept the fact that old age has arrived, it brings a new and exciting challenge. You are then empowered to give the last act of life a truly elegant performance.

Putting a specific number to this point of passage used to be easy. A century or so ago you became old when you celebrated your 65th birthday. That was when men could retire from working, pocket the gold watches their bosses gave them and pick up the fishing rod. No one ever explained why a gold watch is useful to a fisherman. Maybe a gold reel would have been more appropriate. Grandpa probably didn't live long enough to get tired of fishing. He had already exceeded his life expectancy.

Life expectancy is a concept figured out with great precision by mathematical eggheads called actuaries, for purposes like putting a price on a life insurance policy, which must be valued in terms of how long you're likely to remain among us. They can calculate and state with scientific confidence that you who have reached the age of X can now expect to live for Y more years. Thanks to the wonders created by another group of eggheads called the medical profession, we are routinely failing to die on schedule, or to put it another way, out-living our life expectancy. If you know an actuary you might be entitled to drop in, stick out your tongue, and give him a good old "Nanner, Nanner, Nanner". The number of Americans who have passed the 100 mark and still lead active lives is growing fast. Some doctors predict that living to be 120 will be the norm in the not-too-distant future. Many of the earliest retirement homes sold their units as life estates, and soon went belly-up when residents failed to expire as was expected.

That 65th birthday has lost all of its significance, except in relation to Social Security, and no longer does the word retirement represent a highly desirable life of endless leisure. Those who happen to be leaving a long-term position today, either voluntarily or involuntarily, would prefer that you call this transitioning. The word retire does evoke an image of going to bed, whereas what they really are doing is getting up for some new activity, or phase of life. They like to refer to 65 as the "new 45". Some lucky souls feel affluent enough to transition at ages much younger than 65, and many are still employed for many years after that. That greeter at Walmart, long into collecting retirement income, has become an icon. In one large senior community where the entry age was 65 years, a poll showed that about 80% of the residents had some form of employment, volunteer or otherwise.

Recently, at a dinner party, we heard a man state with some pride that he was now semi-retired.

> *"What in the world does semi-retired mean?" another guest asked.*
>
> *"It means he spends half his time on the golf course and the other half resting up in the club bar," his wife replied.*

Numbers are slippery. It seems your chronological age, even though permanently etched on your driver's license and social security card, doesn't serve well to define that critical time when you enter the ranks of old age. We all know people who seem and act much younger than they actually are, and vice versa. My friend George, for example, had mastered the role of cranky old man when he was still in his forties. We sometimes suspected that George was born old. On the other hand nearly every town has at least one woman who is old enough to have great-grandchildren, but still dresses like Little Bo Peep. Some of us might say that the answer could lie in the old saying "You're only as old as you feel." As clichés go, this one probably takes a prize for defying logic!

That being said, isn't it true that a person, with proper stimulation, might feel as frisky as a speckled pup one day and as ancient as an undiscovered tomb the next? My friend Page, for example, decided once that she had reached the western slope, and she played that role for weeks, boring her friends to tears with her recitations of tiresome symptoms. Then, to my astonished eyes, one day I saw her flying down the avenue at reckless speed on <u>roller skates</u> with her latest boy-toy in tow. What's that all about? It's called rejuvenation.

Trying to define that moment in time when one's "last act" begins could strain the brain of the most talented rocket scientist. That very same scientist, while brushing his teeth this morning, may have been looking in the mirror and said to himself "Good Lord, where did that old man come from?!!" Those who remain firmly rooted in a state of denial about having arrived at this stage can probably be forgiven. On the other hand, if you don't choose to notice that the curtain has already gone up, how in the world can you expect to earn curtain calls?

Answering the following set of questions might help in this troublesome diagnosis:

1. Are you winded after walking:

      A. two or three miles.

      B. one mile.

C. to the corner and back.

D. upstairs.

2. Has any one of your potential heirs asked you if you've done your estate planning?

3. Do you check up on friends by a daily perusal of the obituaries?

4. (For men only). Do you face the decision of whether to locate the trousers above or below the tummy?

5. Do merchants bestow the senior discount on you without your asking?

6. Are you ever embarrassed because you can't recall the name of:

A. a recent acquaintance.

B. an old friend.

C. a relative.

D. your spouse.

7. (For women only). Are you afraid that there could be very obvious evidence if you miss your hair-coloring appointment?

8. Do you have an arthritic joint or two that can predict the weather more accurately than the gurus on television?

9. Has anyone had a serious chat with you about surrendering your drivers license?

10. Have you investigated the price of hearing aids?

11. Did you ever lose your eyeglasses, and later find that you had put them in the refrigerator?

12. Do you stop for a rest in the middle of a flight of stairs, and then have to pause and think about whether you were going up or down?

Pondering on honest answers to questions like this probably won't convince the dedicated die-hards who are determined, a la Peter Pan, to stay where they are in life as though the clock isn't ticking. What it might do is give you a reason to wonder if your acquaintances are still apt to describe you as "middle-aged".

CHAPTER 2

DON'T ASK.
DON'T TELL

There may be no social gaffe more horrible than asking a dear little lady who did not wish anyone to know her age, if she would mind telling you how old she is. She will often reply "How old do you think I am?" You may have once skated on thin ice or trod through a land-mine-strewn field of battle, but never before have you been on more dangerous ground than this. No matter how you feel about George Washington and the cherry tree, we strongly recommend using a bold-faced lie in this circumstance. Anything less just won't cut it.

Salesladies in the Midwest often addressed an elderly lady in a friendly manner as "Grandma". This always turned my mother-in-law's face an ugly shade of purple. She didn't even allow her own grandchildren to call her "Grandma". She often said to me, "Remember, my dear, you must not let them put the birth date in my obituary". Her friend Lucinda lied about her age for such a long time that she came to believe her own estimate, and couldn't understand why she was receiving social security checks long before she expected them.

Imagine my surprise, then, at this turn of events. Mom and some of her buddies were sitting on the patio, drinking tea and sharing a discussion about whether the red pills or the blue ones were better for sciatica, and did anyone have some left over so Edna could try them. I distinctly heard her say "You girls better listen to me. I'm going on eighty, you know." Eighty? I happened to know she was only seventy-eight. Well, this sudden change from keeping her age a top secret to blurting it out and even exaggerating is not unusual. Others tell of a similar thing happening in their families. Just exactly when and why it happens is not so clear.

It's understandable that children often speak of "going on". They're going on six not very long after that fifth birthday. That persists year after year as long as it seems that older kids not only have more privileges but also, or so it seems, more fun. (Of course when older kids make false claims to having arrived at eighteen or twenty-one and even acquiring fake ID's to prove it, this may have something to do with being served restorative beverages.)

We have to admit that this opus is already filling up with confusion. In the first chapter we expounded on how difficult it is to define just when one becomes "old". Now we add that there's quite often a point in time when people who were always extremely sensitive and secretive about age seem to have a sudden reversal, and might even view it with pride, but who knows when or if that is going to happen?

When Edith mentioned to me that she had some arthritic pain in one ankle, I ventured onto a slippery slope when I responded, "Well, that does happen to us when we're old." She was outraged, and hastened to tell me she was not old. OK, but in my defense I have to tell you that Edith had recently celebrated her ninety-seventh birthday.

One doesn't have to advance any great distance into adulthood, however, to find that seeming younger beats the heck out of seeming older. (The only exception that comes to mind was Sven. He was bald when he was only 25, so when applying for a job he always said he was 35 so that he could claim having had more experience and thus be paid more.) On the other hand there is Ian, who recently divorced his wife after 35 years. Lately he's been seen around town, escorting a pretty little blonde who looks like she might be a classmate of one of his children. Someone should warn Ian that mortgages and lawns that need mowing and colicky babies don't get easier the second time around!

Clearly, looking and seeming younger is an established goal. If not, why are people spending an ungodly amount of time and money on face lifts, laser treatments, body enhancements, spa visits, hair styling and cosmetic dentistry? Please do not for one minute think that the clients for these services are all women. Men are also likely to recognize that the passage of time can render the human face and frame somewhat less than esthetically pleasing. The aging body, alas, is all too likely to succumb to the force of gravity! As someone remarked, "Time is a great healer, but a lousy beautician".

Why, then, would my mother-in-law, who would have had murderous thoughts about anyone placing the proper number of candles on her birthday cake, now find it more desirable to be "going on eighty" than to be an honest seventy-eight? Whatever the reason, she is certainly not unique. It seems that a good many people who manage to live to what is called "a ripe old age", do one day cross over from pursuing youth and decide to take pride in their longevity. We suspect that most eighty-nine year-olds are "going on ninety"; and when a person is approaching the century mark they are virtually shouting it from the rooftops.

All this would have been very understandable if we lived a century ago.

Life expectancy then was at about fifty years, give or take a few, so the elderly were scarce, but highly esteemed. It was generally thought back then that anyone who had survived for a long period of time had obviously learned a lot and was a fountain of wisdom and knowledge; and was therefore owed a great deal of respect. Unfortunately, this admirable attitude is no longer held by succeeding generations.

Mom tells stories about life on a farm in northern Wisconsin back in the horse-and-buggy days. When one of the children was sick, her mother probably turned to her "doctor book". Every household must have had one. If that didn't tell her what to do for the sick chick, she then sought help from a Grandma. Trying to see a doctor was a last resort. Similarly, if Pop needed advice about a crop or livestock, he would undoubtedly turn to a Grandpa.

Contrast that attitude with the days when the 'Baby Boomers' used to say, "You can't trust anyone over thirty." Of course they've gotten over that now that they're in their sixties. Have we then returned to the role of being their highly respected sources of wisdom? Not likely. If anything, the boomers now see their parents as "problems". The Boomers are often described as being in a sandwich position, squeezed between the weighty responsibilities and high costs of educating their children and the equally expensive cost of caring for their parents.

Now picture this. The Baby Boomer not only fails to see his or her parent as having amassed a useful stock of wisdom, but rather imagines that dementia of old age has arrived or is about to arrive. Conversations often start with "Mom (or Dad), <u>really</u>. Isn't it time that you... blah blah blah ...." Or "We really don't think you should...blah blah blah." Here we have another interesting development that occurs as we age. It is a reversal of the normal parent/child relationship. It may be spawned in love and caring, but old folks who still feel competent to run their own lives find it as welcome as an attack of kidney stones.

One thing you can probably say about the Boomers – they have good manners. They were properly taught by a generation who believed common courtesy goes a long way toward making life on this planet pleasant. It's sad to see that the advent of technological miracles, which has engaged succeeding generations has all but done away with courtesy. A friend tells of seeing her young son, a junior in high school, come into the house and walk right by the chair she was sitting in without a word. He ran up the stairs to his own room and within a few moments she received a text message saying: "When is dinner going to be ready?" We're happy to report she sent back a text reading "Not in your lifetime!"

Trying to establish an ordinary conversation with a youngster in the "Gen Y" or "millenial" generation is a challenge. Being wedded, as they are, to computers, cell phones and the like, they are totally unprepared, and often ill at ease, in face-to-face situations unless, heaven forbid, the subject is technological. Whether you're trying to discuss something fairly serious with them or just to engage in some friendly small talk, you will probably find very little meaningful response. One of my grandkids was gung-ho to demonstrate for me all the functions his new little I-pad could perform. It is debatable which was more obvious, my lack of understanding or my lack of interest in anything he was saying.

What do they think of elderly people? Well, one young man expressed it very concisely. "Anyone who cannot operate a Blackberry or doesn't know how to use one's apps is Medieval." (Sorry, dear reader – I haven't the slightest idea what an app is, much less how to use it.)

So, if the seniors are chronologically challenged, why would some be announcing new peaks of longevity with undeniable pride?   We often heard Mom boast that she had survived all of her siblings. Apparently survival in itself is satisfying, and seniority does earn respect if only in one's own age group.

The story is told of a pastor who asked a group of parishioners to raise their hand if they could recall anyone who had ever done them a dirty trick, and whom they had not forgiven. All but one very old lady, Elly May, raised their hands. Afterwards he went up to her and said. "Elly May, isn't there anyone you feel you should forgive?" "No, sir" she replied. "The bitches are all dead."

So you see that there are some aspects of life on the western slope that are not only satisfying but possibly quite delightful. Read on.

"BUT, MOM... SHE SAID SHE WAS BORN BEFORE TV WAS INVENTED, SO NATURALLY I ASKED HER IF SHE LIVED IN A CAVE BEFORE HOUSES WERE INVENTED."

CHAPTER 3

What's in a Name....

The question before us now is: how does one describe the people who have reached – however you define it – the western slope of life? Surely we can agree that "western slopers" doesn't cut it. It matters what word or phrase you use to describe any special group of human beings because we now live an age that is constantly stressed about "political correctness".

You who feel you have become familiar with an appropriate set of adjectives for special people are bound to find out any day now, that what was O.K. yesterday is now insulting.

Take, for instance, the word "handicapped". It means limited in the ability to perform certain functions, and can apply to hearing, visual, physical and even psychological problems. The United States Congress used this word in formulating the Federal Fair Housing Act which protects, among other groups, the handicapped, which is why we have handicapped parking and handicapped parking stickers, and handicapped accesses, etc. (for which many of us who find these useful are grateful.) Just a few years later that same august body, the Congress, passed the Americans with Disabilities Act, with benefits for the same group, only now handicapped was replaced by "disabled" which means limited in the ability to perform certain functions. Go figure. It wasn't long before "disabled" was also considered to be unkind and possibly harmful to the self respect of the sufferer, so as we write, the new and acceptable word is "challenged". The child who is blind is described as "visually challenged". By that same reasoning, the old folks might then be called "chronologically challenged". This does not strike us as likely to become an acceptable label, because quite a few people balk at six syllable words, but Heaven forbid that we should trample on anyone's self image!

We have also encountered this same sensitivity to the use of adjectives in describing ethnic groups. How many words were first proposed and then later discarded before the name "African-American" became a favorite?

(It may be wise to avoid even that when talking to a dark-skinned young man who plays professional football and who is very proud to have come from the Pacific island of Samoa)

The most remarkable thing about "political correctness is the fact that it seems to have been spawned in younger generations, who are otherwise supremely disinterested in being "proper" and who have staged ruinous attacks on the English language. If a dear old teacher who labored for long hours to teach proper spelling and the art of constructing elegant phrases, sentences and paragraphs should view text messages today, said teacher would undoubtedly be considering suicide.

What is even worse – some of us can recall a time when radio performers knew they would lose their jobs if they used any word that might offend a dear little old, psalm-singing lady from Iowa. There was a man who used to read stories to little children on the radio. One day, unaware that his microphone hadn't been turned off, he was heard to say "that oughta keep the little bastards." He not only lost his job but was unwelcome at any other station or network. Now, as Henry Higgins states in "My Fair Lady", they're using language that would make a sailor blush. Cursing has lost its shock value and is rapidly becoming a bore.

We hope all of this deep thinking about language serves to explain why those of us who have definitely piled on a lot of years, when asked how we'd like our age group to be defined, do not have a ready answer. Perhaps a few editorial comments about terms we do hear will prove helpful.

<u>Old</u> We would have to agree – these three little letters express the truth the whole truth and nothing but the truth. However, you can't avoid seeing it represents a direct opposite to that magic word young. You can bet no aspiring ad executive, in writing marketing material for a real estate development the client is creating for older people will use this word. Handle with care..

<u>Old folks</u> The word "old" acquires a rustic touch by adding the "folks" part. This may render it a tad more acceptable but only, we suspect, to unsophisticated people who have piled on quite a few years.

<u>Curmudgeon</u> An old-fashioned word commonly used to describe a person who has become unfailingly cranky. Interestingly enough, this seems to be used only to describe men. Unfortunately, curmudgeons rarely seem to realize that they are indeed cranky so will not react favorably.

<u>Codger</u> just a tad more friendly than a curmudgeon.

<u>Has-been</u> Possibly better than "never-was", but definitely implies "no-longer-is". Not likely to create a friendly climate if used face-to-face. However, we do encounter now and then an individual who is prepared to expound by the hour about the great career they once had. Whether the claim is believable or not, this may be the phrase that will enter your mind. Keep it there.

<u>Retiree</u>　May be accurate, but this word no longer enjoys the happy "time-to-smell-the-roses" image it once had. There are some　people who announce with great pleasure that they have "retired" and plan to do nothing but relax and enjoy life for the　rest of their days.　I doubt if that plan lasts more than a few weeks before boredom intervenes. "Leisure" is a good word　because it offers options.　I vote to remove the word "retire" and　all its' spin-offs from our vocabulary. Developer, Del Webb,　was brilliant when he named his retirement communities　 "Leisure World".

<u>Old Coot</u>　Even dedicated Scrabble players rarely can tell you what the word "coot" means.　Our research indicates it is some type of　duck.　There was a time when the word "ducky" was used affectionately, but that was a long time ago.　We do recall that "cooties" used to mean head lice, so for that reason alone, you might want to would avoid this phrase.

<u>Senior</u>　Means "older' and does convey some respect in the　academic world. It also describes the 4th year students in high　school, but the chances of any confusion as to whether it is being　used to designate them or us is certainly minimal. We　outnumber them, so can probably use this title at will. "Senior　friendly community" is the wording that ad executive who had to　find a phrase for describing a developer's project uses a lot.

Senior citizen   A bit more formal and generally used when seeking some special right accorded to senior citizens. This is our title when used by AARP and other lobbyists who hassle Congress for our Social Security and Medicare rights. I cherish my tee shirt that reads:

"Senior Citizen. Where's my damned discount?"

Geezer   Like "curmudgeon" an old-fashioned word and not very respectful. Somehow, though, we always feel it has a warm- fuzzy personality. Years ago I ran across a wonderfully funny little book about becoming a "geezer", and bought a dozen or so copies. It made a perfect birthday gift for anyone turning 65.

Emeritus   A title of distinction earned by one who has had a distinguished career, but one can hardly call people "emerituses" or "emeriti"!

Blue hairs   The use of this sort of phrase identifies the speaker as being rude, disrespectful, and totally uninformed about modern hair- coloring techniques. We are also sometimes referred to as gray- hairs or white-hairs, but if expecting a friendly reception, it would be wise to avoid references to hair. Too many of us are down to little or none.

Elderly   Has the same simple meaning as 'old', but maybe three syllables soften it just a tad. I use it both as an adjective and as a noun. (My computer's grammar-check function gets huffy about that, but defying the computer is one of my favorite indoor sports.)

Some years ago a team of government inspectors were making their annual visit to a home for retarded children. They met with the Executive Director of the home when they had finished and praised him for having an exceptionally well-run facility.

"But," one of the inspectors asked, "how come so many of your employees look like they must be already on social security?"

"Well, you see", he replied, "these children need a lot of loving.

Some of then are not that easy to love. I'm always glad when I get the opportunity to employ a <u>post graduate parent</u>."

"NO, MELISSA..., YOU MAY <u>NOT</u> REFER TO YOUR BELOVED GRANDPARENTS AS 'THE OLD-FARTS!' IF I HEAR THAT ONE MORE TIME, YOU'LL BE GROUNDED UNTIL NINE DAYS AFTER THE SECOND COMING!"

CHAPTER 4

The Weather Predictors

In a water aerobics class at a senior center, the instructor once asked, in a conversational tone, if anyone in the group suffered aches in a joint when the weather changed. After a roar of laughter, one member of the group explained to her that she should have asked if anyone did NOT have a joint pain or two when the weather changed.

There is no denying that an old person, climbing out of bed in the morning and making that how-do-I-feel today self assessment can often identify a few pesky issues. Unless you're one of those persons who dote on each ache and pain, and will share them in conversation with anyone who will listen - most of these issues disappear if you take an aspirin and take satisfaction in the fact that you're still on the right side of the sod.

As we well know, the parts of your trusty automobile wear out after a certain number of miles driven, striking joy into the hearts of the mechanics and the new-car dealers who rely on that for their livelihood.

Arthritis is the name for that same wear and tear we sustain on our movable parts – knees, hips, shoulders and ankles – after decades of hard use. In this case it is the orthopedic surgeon who rejoices. He can replace that joint and in doing so might earn enough to pay for at least one semester of his son's path through college. Since arthritis can hurt like the very dickens, it is also enriching the purveyors of pain medications. (We do enjoy pointing out that even retirees make a significant contribution to the economy!) The lucky souls who escape arthritis are so few in number that one sometimes wonders if the good Lord was not in favor of human beings walking on only two legs. Maybe it's a thing we thought up ourselves and are paying the price?

Another bugaboo for seniors, and fairly common, is osteoporosis. This fancy set of syllables describes the condition that occurs when bones that were once very strong and well able to support the body, have become chalky, brittle and all-too-likely to break. This condition can even reach a point where a coughing fit can produce a fracture! Stairs and ramps become hazardous. (Now there are preventive medications, which taken over time, can often prevent osteoporosis – probably not so commonly prescribed when today's older generation were younger.)

We often see people who are only middle-aged, holding the phone book out at the maximum extent of an arm so that they can read the fading print. Vision, then, is another one of those abilities we might take for granted in our youth; but which can start to fade in later years. Eye glasses become standard equipment. It doesn't improve with old age.

A new employee in a senior center complained that no one was reading the notices she posted in the elevators. The poor girl didn't realize we don't wear our reading glasses in the elevator.

So far this sorry list includes aching joints, brittle bones and fuzzy vision. Now add to the list muscles that have lost strength and reflexes that have slowed down to the pace of a dyspeptic turtle; and we have a recipe for falling. Elderly people fall down A LOT. They fall indoors and outdoors, over rugs, curbs etc. and even often fall out of bed. Bathtubs and showers are particularly hazardous. When they fall they usually have a broken bone or two. We heard that at a senior facility which houses over two thousand residents, an ambulance is always waiting at the door, and when it pulls away another takes its place. Plaster casts and slings are the latest fashion statement in the senior world

Of course there are exceptions. For example, I went looking for our Mom one day to ask her about some arrangements for her ninetieth birthday party. She wasn't in her apartment and her neighbor said she thought she'd gone looking for some plums to make jam. Do you think that means she's at the grocery store? Heavens, NO! I found her perched in the lower branches of a plum tree happily filling her basket with fresh fruit.

Mom's way of life reminds us of a man who once said "If I'd known how long I was going to live, I'd have paid more attention to staying in shape!" The rules are painfully simple – keep moving and stay thin. There are some people who can never push themselves away from the dining-room table, especially if there's a gooey chocolate dessert in the offing. And also some who avoid any exercise more strenuous than lifting a teacup or a martini. It's too bad, but these are the ones whose bodies are crying out for some hours on an exercise bike or treadmill.

Speaking of our disabilities, I seem to have read once that people as they age spend less and less time and money on doctors. It doesn't seem logical unless you realize how drastically medical practices have changed since our youth. The "family doctor" who made "house calls" is now rarer than the dodo bird. I still recall the year one of my kids was bedridden for two weeks, and the wonderful doctor who stopped by every day on his way to his office. He usually showed up very early in the morning, so brought in the milk bottles and turned on the coffee on his way to the bedside.

Now it is difficult to find <u>any</u> doctor who will take a patient in Medicare unless you pay a big extra fee for his service. Nor can you ever talk to a <u>real person</u> on this phone. When you finally get to meet this doctor you find yourself with a man who is about the same age as your youngest grandchild. No wonder our Mom used to say, "I don't want anything to do with those young whippersnappers". No wonder we seniors soon decide that all these modern diagnostic tests just lead to learning things you didn't want to know anyhow. When my friend Wilbur was told he might need a knee replacement he replied "Don't worry doctor, I'm rubbing holy water on it and it's getting along just fine."

Among the things for which we seniors can envy the young, is the ability to fall into bed and sleep like a log until the alarm clock rings. Most of us old folks are not good sleepers. If it isn't snoring or muscle cramps or heart burn, it's those inevitable one-or-more trips to the john. Lack of sleep may be one reason why depression is sometimes an unwelcome visitor. It is also the reason many older couples opt for separate bedrooms. (Young people tend to look very sad when I mention this, so I hasten to add that it certainly doesn't mean that they no longer care – they can and probably do <u>visit.)</u>

The number of senior citizens who avail themselves of hearing aids is pretty large, and we have to admit that there are also quite a few who should use aids but don't. Science has gone a long way to make the aids so small as to be almost unnoticed. However, some other problems do remain:

The hearing aids are unbelievably expensive.
They operate on tiny batteries that are forever running out of juice.

The owners are forever running out of batteries.
It is not unusual to find oneself shouting at someone because they either forgot to insert the hearing devices, or have temporarily mislaid them.

Sadly, the need to raise one's voice to the level of a hog-calling contest, especially in a room full of people, is decidedly annoying. When you deliver one of your funniest stories, and amongst some laughter, hear "WHAT WAS THAT? I DIDN'T HEAR YOU. WOULD YOU REPEAT THAT PLEASE." your patience is stretched thin. Sometimes you wonder if it is really a hearing problem or a case of inattention. (Public speakers agree that attendees who complain that they cannot hear are invariably seated in the back row, and firmly refuse to move to vacant seats up front!) On the other hand there are people whose voices are so tiny that the sound never gets beyond the front teeth.

It may surprise you to know that hearing disabilities are often more difficult to adjust to than visual. If visiting a person who uses a hearing aid, perhaps the most important rule is to avoid situations where you're competing with a lot of background noise. If for example you're taking an elderly person out for dinner, avoid restaurants where music and/or conversation is bouncing off hard surfaces to a decibel level that is almost painful. (That may eliminate half the eateries in town!) Small groups for social occasions are best, so speakers are not competing for attention.

Hearing aid users will almost always prefer that you NOT shout at them. If you face them when you are speaking so that they can see your lips, pronounce words clearly and avoid a machine-gun style of delivery, you should be understood.

The effect that hearing problems have on elderly communication is interesting. Assume you have three senior citizens involved in a conversation. It might go somewhat like this:

1st person: "I just heard Larry's transferred to France."
2nd person "Why ever would Garry want furry pants?"

3rd person "What's this about Mary's bayberry plants?"

Younger people who read these words of wisdom about hearing disabilities had better pay close attention. Their love affair with decibels, leading to music (?) played at the sound level of an explosion in a boiler factory, is predicted to result in many more hearing handicaps, experienced earlier and earlier in life.

A lot of young people seem to think that anyone who has gray hair either has Alzheimer's disease, or is about to have it. The fact is that extreme cases of dementia from any cause are not inevitable. Many seniors in their 80's, 90's or even past the 100 mark can still do the New York Times crossword puzzle in ink – and still prepare their own income tax returns. What senior citizens do commonly suffer from is <u>near memory loss.</u> Names of people, streets, places, etc. do not trip merrily off the tongue the way they used to. Picture four elderly people having a chat about old movies, and not one could recall the name of the actor who was the star. Probably three would be awakened in the night by a phone call and a joyous shout from the fourth participant "It was GARY COOPER!" Better late than never.

It does happen that memory loss can occur, even at much earlier stages of life. The better half of a couple in their late forties tells about her husband's problem with names. She says that if they're going to have dinner with friends, before meeting them he'll be saying "What's what-his-name's wife's name?" So why should you be surprised that Grandma can't remember the name of the street she used to live on, or repeats something she just said five minutes ago?

Please do not ascribe any one in this litany of woes to any older person you know unless you have good reason to do so. We feel sure that no one suffers from all of them, and some people don't suffer from any of them. A young lady tells a delightful story about her 92-year-old Granny. Granny lived in a small town and occupied a two-story house she had owned for sixty years. Family members used to live in this town but gradually they had drifted away, so now no one was looking after Granny. She couldn't be persuaded to move, but they breathed a sigh of relief when a 60-year-old niece who had taken early retirement moved in with Granny. A year later a daughter visited Granny and discovered that the niece had suffered a stroke, and was partially paralyzed. Granny was not only managing to take care of herself, but also doing a fine job of caring for her caregiver!

Our Mom was ninety-five when she moved into an assisted care facility. I visited her one day and took her for a drive. When we got back to her place I asked her where she wanted to be. In the dining hall, or lounge or in her apartment, etc.? She replied "Take me to the smoking room."

"Mom, you've never smoked in your life and you sure aren't going to start now," I cried.

"I know I don't smoke, she went on, "but that's where the men are."

"ETHEL, I'M SURE THAT WOMAN OVER THERE WAS IN OUR CLASS. WHAT WAS HER NAME?"

"HOW SOON DO YOU NEED TO KNOW?"

CHAPTER 5

Sounding Strategic Retreat

We feel obliged to follow up the litany of aches and pains in the previous chapter with a description of some of the life-style changes that will probably result. Unless the sufferer has been a dedicated couch potato already, disabilities usually call for adjustments. On a happier note, some lucky souls never have these issues. I remember having lunch with three of my uncles many years ago. They were all in their eighties. Uncle Jack was sailing the next week for a grand tour of Europe. Uncle Harry had just published another book, and Uncle Fred was heading for Florida to visit one of his ex-wives. They were enjoying life to the max.

Winter ski vacations used to be events I looked forward to with great enthusiasm despite a pitiful lack of skill. The day did come, however, when people started saying "Are you SURE you should be doing this at your age? The answer to that question became pretty obvious when I began to feel as if the ski patrol was dusting off their stretcher the moment they saw me hit the slopes. Fractures are painful. It was time for a retreat.

My tennis game staged a more gradual exit. First I switched from singles to doubles, and then later found myself yelling "YOURS" at my partner whenever the ball didn't seem to be cooperating. Now the rackets are collecting dust. It may be late in life for me to take up golf, but the idea that one can ride around in a cart is enticing. Is it possible that old golfers never retreat?

Emma is an elderly lady who is determined to stay on her feet even though her ability to walk is now limited to pushing one foot a wee bit ahead of the other to gain about four inches per step. When urged to use a wheel chair or perhaps at least a walker, she stubbornly refuses. "That would be a retreat," she says, "and I am not ready to give an inch in this battle." You have to admire her spirit and hope that her ability may improve, even though having some doubts about her common sense.

A truly traumatic adjustment rears its ugly head when it comes to our use of an automobile. One gentleman we know was not only past ninety, but totally deaf, and blind in one eye – but still not inclined to give up driving. When his drivers license was up for renewal we felt sure that would take care of this matter, but to our amazement, it was renewed and he promptly bought a new car.

You can never underestimate the love affair the average American has with his or her automobile. Even the weakest and wussiest body feels POWERFUL behind the wheel. The ability to make the car go wherever you want it to go is more than just transportation. It represents our independence!

Miranda's driving became so erratic that her family took her car keys away from her – but she had an extra set. Then they parked an old snow plow in front of her garage so that she couldn't get her car out. She promptly went out and bought another car. This gives you some idea of how strongly some seniors feel about their cars. It also reminds you to pull off the road when you see them coming! As they say in Florida "If all you can see is the hands on top of the wheel of that car coming toward you, take cover."

Our Mom was seventy years old when her beloved husband passed away. Until then, Pop was always the driver and she was the navigator in their powerful Buick. After she took the wheel it was only a couple of weeks before she had a minor accident in the parking area behind a small office building we owned. She put a dent in our secretary's parked car. No problem. We had it fixed. Fast forward to a short time later, a second incident. She hit the same car again with the same result. While we were dealing with that embarrassment, she managed to attract police attention by rear-ending another lady's car. This, she insisted, was not her fault because they were stopped at a stop light, and when the light turned green, the other lady didn't go right away. "I had a GREEN light" she cried. We thought they might take her license away, but no, they only required that she take a safe driving course.

The end came when she phoned me one day saying "Don't tell anyone, but please send me a carpenter. I had a small problem pulling into my garage and one wall needs some repair." Needless to say, I hurried to her apartment where I saw that their three-car garage had been practically totaled. The Buick was still operable, but had enough dimples to look like a golf ball. I took her car away and opened a charge account for her at a local taxi company so that she could use their services any time – hoping that would appease her. No such luck. It was some time before our loving relationship lost its chill.

Now my own children are starting to get "parental" about my driving, and I do know they're motivated by caring, but that does not dispose me to be inclined to accept their advice and give it up. No, not yet. I do admit (not to them) that

I am tending to avoid driving at night or in rainy weather, and would have to agree that I don't back up very well, but how often do you have to back up? Not very.

We come now to the scariest of transitions. That comes when you discover that you can no longer manage one or more of the really essential chores without some help. You can no longer cut your toenails or put on your shoes and socks. You forget whether you took your medicine or not. Getting lost or tending to lose your balance are becoming daily issues. You can see, or are being told, that you need part-time or full time caregiver help.

Maybe you know someone like our former neighbor whom we called "the Admiral". His doctor told him he needed nursing care, His family dutifully hired nurses, but not one of them lasted a full day before the irascible old gentleman showed them the door. He was also supposed to walk with a cane, but usually trotted around waving the cane over his head.

In the senior facility where I live, my apartment is in a section called "independent living". There is also a section for "assisted care" and another for "memory support" and still another for "skilled nursing". Those of us in independent living are free to come and go as we choose. To be honest, it's not exactly the life style you had when you lived in your own home. There are a few rules related to community living and safety. For example, we have to sign out if we're going to be away overnight because there is a device on each apartment door which alerts the staff if you haven't opened your door by 11 A.M. - obviously for our protection.

Moving from independent living to one of the higher levels of care is locally described as "going over". Some people seem to have a talent for realizing that they need to do that, or accept it when advised by family or staff, and make the change quite seamlessly, enjoying their new environment. I suspect, though, that many of us, wisely or not, regard it as welcome as banishment to Siberia and fight tooth and nail. You can avoid going over if you have a dedicated spouse who can and will provide care, or the means to hire a private care-giver.

You have to feel deep sympathy for loving relatives when they are forced by circumstances to make these tough decisions for us against our bitter opposition. Mildred's daughters were devoutly hoping for the best when they bodily moved their mother from their house to an apartment where assisted care was available. Mildred locked her apartment door and refused to come out for weeks. They had to leave groceries on her doorstep so that she wouldn't starve. Her mental condition deteriorated rapidly and at last the apartment management moved her into a nursing home. I asked a nurse if she was doing better there, and she replied "Mildred bites."

The good news is, the oldest generation is growing so fast in numbers that there is a boom in the creation of "senior friendly" facilities designed for the care of the elderly including those needing physical or mental support. Within these you may find a dedicated staff of loving people who provide entertainment, games, "happy hours", and anything else they can think of, along with the care needed. That can't be all bad.

In describing the life style issues we face when disabilities arise with age, we debated using the word "retreat" vs. "transition" or "adjustment".

All of these could apply, but the phrase "strategic retreat" sounded best to us because it implies CHOICE. As we see it, a lifetime is full of choices, and it is not the issues we face that impact us, but the choices we make when we face the issues. For example, when you have to give up one favorite activity, you can whine and complain about that for the rest of your days, or you can search for a workable substitute. One old lady we know who can no longer walk, is now taking piano lessons and loving it!

You can bet your loved ones will give you a big round of applause if you make the choices yourself in a timely manner, before they're forced to make them for you. After all, a retreat is NOT a form of surrender. No, not at all.

"GET A MOVE ON, HERBERT. I HAVE TO DRIVE YOU TO THE SENIOR CENTER AND YOU KNOW I LIKE TO DRIVE AT RUSH HOUR... THEY GO SO NICE AND SLOW."

CHAPTER 6

Smelling Those Roses

Believe it or not, certified members of the white-haired (or no-haired) generation can testify that there are some very good things about this stage of life. We must qualify that rash statement by admitting that good things tend to happen to people who expect good things to happen, so it's important that this chapter prove to be positive and convincing. Those who embrace a negative slant on everything probably feel cheated when a day fails to produce a reason to gripe. Negativity is a vicious, communicable disease and elderly people are wise to avoid anyone who is so afflicted!

Consider, for example, Loretta, who moved into a certain senior center; after living in three other similar facilities in succession, each of which proved to be unsatisfactory in one way or another. No one was greatly surprised when, only five months later, Loretta was once again relocating. Someone remarked that if Loretta ever got to Heaven (which was not thought to be likely) she would no doubt find it featured some unacceptable deficiencies.

Frugal folks who have made sure of an adequate retirement income can enjoy an enchanting variety of new ways to spend their time. Unfortunately, that often requires that responsible decisions were made about thirty or forty years ago whereas some did not get into worrying about retirement income until last week. However, even people who discover that the social security check is not very elastic, and who cannot or do not want to ask for help from family, might find convenient, no-stress jobs. Happily, many employers are discovering that older workers are wonderfully reliable. Some merchants are happy to provide hours and circumstances to fit the retiree's needs. Part time work carrying little responsibility can actually be quite enjoyable.

"It's as if I've been running to catch a train all my life," one man explained, "and now I can slow down to a walk and even stop for a rest here and there." No more alarm clock to start the day. I don't even wear a watch. No more hatchet-faced boss to please, no more boring meetings, no more impossible clients, no more ladder to climb. One lady described the change in her life when she became elderly by saying "I no longer have to have anything to do with high maintenance people." Ambition is not the name of the game now.

My goals in life may not be very challenging any more, but they are definitely delightful. Relationships become much more meaningful when constraints of time and energy lead to weeding out those that were mostly obligatory and less that satisfying. It's just too bad if that hatchet-faced cousin thinks I should call her every week. Recalling old times with truly good friends, though, is a joy, and especially if you're blessed with siblings who share memories of your childhood. A phone call or visit from one of my old college buddies is good for at least an hour of happy chatter about that goofy professor we had in our biology class, and the time five of us played hooky and hitch-hiked to Washington to see the cherry blossoms. Something truly wonderful happens when a bunch of old World War II veterans get together over a pitcher or two of beer to swap stories.

Seniors also enjoy many tangible benefits in the form of those wonderful senior citizen discounts. Merchants in supermarkets, and department stores usually have discount days for the elderly. Tickets for entertainment venues often come cheaper. Even property taxes might well contain a significant write-off.

As we have indicated, young people today no longer look upon older people as fountains of wisdom and good advice. Respect for the elderly and even common courtesy are sometimes lacking, but have not totally disappeared. "I couldn't travel if it were not for the kindness of strangers," one 90-year-old lady avowed. "There's always at least one person who will stand up to give me a seat, help lift my bag into the overhead compartment, or even lend me an arm to lean on." One old man stated that being old was great because "young girls who wouldn't give me the time of day when I was young, now give me hugs and kisses. I may not be rich or smart, but I'm lovable!"

A good friend and frequent traveling companion of mine, who is many years younger than I am accuses me of "playing the old age card". I must admit to doing that now and then. I have in fact mastered the art of looking pitiful when it can help. The truth is, this friend uses the "card" too. If we're standing in a line she'll go to the front and say "I have this elderly lady with me and she's beginning to feel faint. Can you help us?"

With a little bit of luck, seniors receive and appreciate the priceless gift of time while they still have enough energy to do things they always wanted to do – but couldn't because of the demands of family and economic needs. In a typical lifetime, you spend years pleasing others. You were somebody's child, somebody's spouse, somebody's parent, somebody's employee etc.   It isn't till later in life that you really discover your own identity, - and get to follow your own individual star.

One happy man who was a college professor until retirement is now raising prize orchids. He is also learning a foreign language and taking piano lessons. A group of seniors raised enough money to build a Habitat for Humanity house, and then built it themselves. It's not unusual to hear of some talented individual who published a first book or painted a first salable painting after reaching old age. The mother who had always wanted to be a nurse, is now volunteering in the hospital and loving it. If there is one obvious characteristic that happy elderly people today share, it is that they seem to stay busy.

There's a comfortable sense of satisfaction just in the fact that one has survived all of life's ups and downs for eighty or more years. The media are fond of blasting us with dire warnings about foods we shouldn't be eating or products we shouldn't use; but why should we worry when we've been eating that stuff and using those things for a lifetime, and are still getting along just fine? For some reason Grandma Murphy's doctor had her on a diet that forbid her eating red meat or drinking anything alcoholic. Finally, on her 90th birthday, she announced that she was through with that nonsense. She then continued to include beef and bourbon in her daily rations until her death eleven years later. Her son says her health didn't suffer, and her disposition was decidedly improved. Seniors secretly laugh at the amount of money their kids spend on bottled water. The old folks may carry water bottles too but you can bet they're filled with tap water. It works just fine.

Maybe you've heard it said that old people get away

with murder We haven't put that to a test, but feel there may be at least a kernel of truth in it. Seniors do have a sense of <u>entitlement.</u> There was an old saying that "to those to whom much was given, of these much is expected." Now they might say "I gave, so now I expect to receive!" They've paid their dues – done their life's work - so now are free to say and do whatever floats their boat. No doubt their children may sometimes find this attitude to be downright scary.

We met a 93-year-old lady on a Mediterranean cruise. She was traveling alone, and said gleefully that her children were very upset about that plan. "What if you died over there in Europe?" they asked. "I told them if that happened, I wouldn't be any deader than if I died in Boston."

Memories provide another satisfaction in our declining years. It is probably true that most seniors cannot recall what they had for dinner last night, and unless they wrote down the appointment they're supposed to keep tomorrow, the odds are they won't make it. The memory tapes that were put in place further back, though, are still there and in fact they improve with time. With a little bit of luck we manage to deal with and erase the bad times, while the good times just get better with age. If that weren't true, how come we heard a widow say "Joe and I were married for 60 years and there was never an unkind word." Her sister just smiles and says they used to have shouting matches that could be heard several counties away!

In my old home-and-family days there was not enough time in the day to get all the important stuff done. The clock was a mortal enemy. I was always prioritizing. If, while driving to pick up kids at the school, I happened to see that a wonderful little dogwood tree had just burst into bloom, stopping to admire those precious flowers was out of the question. Imagine having to tell the kids, "Sorry I'm late, guys, but I had to stop and look at a tree." Isn't it an irony that now that I've reached a point where there's far less time left in my life span, I can lavish it on a perfect blossom to my heart's content. You can find pure joy in pausing to appreciate the "little things", a well told story, a delicious dinner or the smell of a lovely rose.

"WHEN I TOLD PA TO TAKE TIME TO SMELL THE ROSES, I DIDN'T MEAN HE SHOULD HANG OUT ALL DAY AT ROSIE'S SALOON."

CHAPTER 7

Significant Others

The phrase "significant others" is not a favorite of mine. It seems to be used frequently to describe a relationship I refer to as "unholy unmatrimony". (Yes, kids, I do know that there's plenty of that going on, but I don't have to approve.) However, the phrase serves to bring up the subject of relationships. It certain is true that "others" are significant. Generally speaking people, with the possible exception of a few long-bearded hermits who inhabit the wilderness, may even find them to be essential. There's an old saying that we need three hugs a day to survive and five to grow. Even though, in the course of raising a large family, I have valued a bit of "alone time" above the crown jewels and still do, I would have to agree that people need people. Recently, the news followed the inspiring story of a large group of miners in Chile, who survived in good shape when confined underground for more than a month. Do you think that if one man had been trapped alone he would have been so fortunate? I wonder.

A truly good marriage seems to be the Lord's own recipe for enduring happiness. The couple whose relationship has survived all ups and downs over a long period of time now know each other's strengths and weaknesses, likes and dislikes. They provide each other with love and affection – and, yes, may even still enjoy sex. (For some reason young people who can lap up pornographic movies find this shocking - Grandma and Grandpa shouldn't do that?) It's fun to see how that couple who have been together for fifty years or more can read each other's minds, finish each other's sentences, and send messages across a crowded room with the twitch of an eyebrow.

Yes, we know that a sad number of marriages don't work out well but the good ones are so very good when viewed from the prospective of many years, that you wonder why so many people mess up relationships for selfish reasons, or simply avoid the altar. Today's divorce statistics are so horrendous that some people are now speculating that weddings may soon become obsolete, Heaven forbid!

Even when one party to that good marriage suffers a serious physical of mental disability, and the other is forced into the role of caregiver, it's inspiring to see how lovingly and tenderly that care us administered. We even see cases where both parties have problems. Rheumatoid arthritis took away my friend Pat's ability to walk very far, and her husband lost his vision to macular degeneration. "He's my legs," she said, "and I am his eyes".

The flip side of this coin rests in the fact that the happy couple rarely make their exits simultaneously, so now comes the grief and the loneliness of the widow/widower role. Some widows feel lost without a man to lean on and start looking for a new candidate quite soon. Unfortunately, they don't find the odds (single men vs. single women) decidedly encouraging. Others, far from being on a man-hunt, have a "been there, did that" attitude. Quite a few find single status a satisfactory role. "After all," Rosemary told her friends, "you can now eat crackers in bed and scratch where it itches," It is also the ultimate solution to the troublesome old toilet-set controversy.

Although possibly prejudiced, I do think widowers have a more difficult time with the grief period. In due time, however, a man whose good wife has always taken care of his home, children, health and his social life is like Hal who cries "I've always been a couple. I don't know how to be anything but that." The chances are pretty good that he'll find a new helpmate. Readers shouldn't be surprised to know that true love can dawn at any age. It isn't unusual for a wedding reception to take place in a senior center.

Our children are another kind of significant other, and they can indeed be a blessing. Offspring who visit often or at least stay in touch, help out now and then and genuinely care for us are a joy beyond measure. I do admit that those old souls who are childless can take some comfort in knowing that there are times when children are a mixed blessing, We hope and strive that they'll get a good education, make a decent living, live a clean life, stay out of jail and marry the right sort of person – i.e. someone we might have chosen for them. We pray for those things but when our prayers are not answered we weep a few tears, sprout a few more gray hairs, and go right on loving the rascals.

It is extremely gratifying when our children produce grandchildren – who are invariable adorable. This affords us the double pleasure of experiencing again the joy of having a little one in your arms, and also the pleasure of being able to hand the tot back to the parent when it becomes tiring. Grandparenting is a spectator sport, and it is frustrating now and then when, for example, you feel like a football fan who thinks the quarterback is making a mess of things. Can any of us resist a good laugh, though, when seeing a little imp give a parent, (your child) some of the same kind of grief he or she used to give to you?

Today, some of our more disturbing social trends have led to a growing number if grandparents faced with not only enjoying their grandkids but also raising them. Most of us would do that when it proves to be necessary, but in the cases I've observed, they are silently shouting NOT FAIR.

Well, most family relationships are sources of great satisfaction to the seniors, but the family feud can be just the opposite. Sibling rivalries, ancient grievances, in-law problems, and the almighty dollar are often the root issues that cause a ton of heartaches. Sometimes you encounter a person who has not had contact with a sibling for years – and you find that the cause of the rift was so minor that neither party can remember exactly what it was! Blessed be the Peacemakers!

Significant others can also be friends. We seniors can certainly enjoy the company of younger people, but it is hard to beat those trips down memory lane that you can have with people of your own vintage, We can revisit the rigors of the Great Depression and agree that no other downturn since can even begin to compare. What young person today knows what it means to "turn a collar"? My contemporaries know. When Dad's shirt collar became frayed, Mom carefully detached it from the shirt, turned it over and reattached it. They couldn't afford a new shirt.

In any gathering a senior citizens, if veterans of World War II are asked to stand, most of the men will rise and a good many of the women. In no conflict since then have the stakes been so high or the response so magnificent. Tom Brokaw may have exaggerated just a little but when he called us "The Greatest Generation", but our soldiers did enter that war against the odds, with a determination to settle for no less that victory, and victory was what they got.

Children will be shocked when their grandparents share some of the facts of life in the "old days". Here are a few when-I-was-a-child items guaranteed to amaze them.

****Our house didn't have a micro-wave oven, air conditioning, or a clothes dryer. Wash was hung on a "clothes line" in the back yard to dry.

****Doctors made "house calls". Penicillin had not yet been discovered and many kids died of typhoid fever, diphtheria, and infantile paralysis.

****Food was kept cold in our house in an "ice box". A man delivered a huge cake of ice each week and placed it in the box.

****We didn't have TV. Movies were silent, and early radios could only get two or three stations – not even that when the weather didn't cooperate. Storms caused static. Early in the evening the radio played the national anthem and went off the air till morning.

****For married women the most likely career was home-making. We didn't have preschools or day care. Unmarried women usually became teachers or nurses.

****During the Great Depression there were few if any government welfare programs. Poor people were helped by "soup kitchens" run by churches and private charities, Some people starved to death.

**** "Grass" was green stuff my Dad had to mow, and the only power the mower had was muscle. "Pot" was one of Mom's cooking utensils.

**** There was a time when having alcoholic beverages was against the law. Even beer was illegal.

**** We never heard of car-jacking, home invaders, or child predators. Our home was never locked and we didn't have a key. Kids walked to school and played outdoors.

**** During World War II gasoline was strictly rationed as were many other foods and products needed for the war production. We couldn't buy nylon stockings so working girls painted their legs.

**** We never heard of tape decks, or software. Fast food was what you couldn't eat during Lent.

**** A postage stamp cost three cents. Two dimes would do for a movie and a snack.

**** In high school and even in college, very few kids had cars. We rode buses.

"MARYBETH, WE'RE SUPPOSED TO SHARE. IF YOU'VE TAKEN ALL THE PRUNES AGAIN, I'M GOING TO REPORT YOU."

CHAPTER 8

Be It Ever So Humble

It is difficult to generalize about what kind of home best suits the seniors. Lifestyles, affordability, family relationships and health issues can all be variables. In the old days an elderly person who ran out of money and had no family support wound up in the county "Home" – also called the "poor house". It was usually somewhere between bad and awful, which is why that word "home", which otherwise has warm connotations, is rarely found in the names of retirement communities. My mother-in-law used to say "Don't worry about me when I get old – just put me in the Home". If we'd taken that seriously, Lord help us!

Despite the fact that our society has been getting more mobile for some time, some people grow old in a house they've occupied for decades. There are probably marks on the kitchen wall where the kids got measured every year as they grew – memories in every brick and board. How many times has Papa mowed that lawn, and how many loads of dirty dishes has Mama handled in the kitchen? Their roots have been dug in deep and it is quite possible that they'll stay in that house, however inconvenient it might have become, forever. As one Realtor put it: "When I look at a house owned by someone over eighty years old, I expect that they've been there for forty years, and there's a moose head over the fireplace."

Old houses, however, - even though they may house many fond memories - have a way of becoming pretty burdensome. They probably have stairs, and stairs are unkind to arthritic knees. Old heating and cooling systems become very temperamental. Costs of repairs, insurance and property taxes keep rising, and the work required to keep the place up increases, just when your own income and energy are moving in the opposite direction. One owner of an older home once remarked "When ever I have a few extra dollars in my wallet, this house seems to know it and finds a way to spend it." If the house doesn't fail to please, it may be that the neighborhood has changed and become less desirable.

For one reason or another, the lure of moving into a newer and more efficient abode begins to call.

You can take it from a lady who spent a good many years helping people buy and sell houses, that helping the elderly couple to make a change may require an awesome amount of patience. They have lots of possibilities to consider and plenty of time to make decisions. What is worse, they have probably acquired a veritable army of people who will help (?) them to make choices. The first big roadblock is the "where-do-we-put-the-children-and-grandchildren   when-they-come-to-visit" question. In my opinion, a nearby motel would work just fine; but maybe they fear that the kids just won't even come to visit if they can't be staying in the familiar old house.

An even larger problem may come up -- the what-to-do-with things. Chances are that if they've been married for more than thirty years they have accumulated enough personal property to fill a sizable warehouse, stashed away in vacant rooms, attics or basements. It's been very truly said that people can own things and that things can own people. A well-known interior decorator once remarked that she had never seen a home in the United States, that wouldn't benefit by hauling away a full truckload of stuff. Lifestyles are changing and it seems that the children really don't want most of the stuff we're saving to hand down to them, but many of us find that hard to believe.

The strong desire to retain the concert grand piano or Grandma's enormous dining room set rules out many houses that might have suited them. And don't we all know of at least one genuine "pack rat" who is emotionally incapable of parting with any little thing they own, however useless it might be? We shudder to think about how many people are paying for the rental on storage facilities that are full of items they'll never want to see again.

These issues may explain why many people in the "baby boomer" generation who became "empty nesters" in their sixties, not that we consider this old, did decide, when making a move, to trade up to houses that were not only newer and more efficient but also much bigger and more expensive, instead of opting for economy. It's more likely they just felt that they had reached a point when they could afford the "house we always dreamed of". They triggered the building boom in "McMansions". A large dose of recession which has caused many retirement incomes to shrink like a bargain-basement t-shirt, may have led to a re-valuation of this trend.

All this often adds up to the fact that that lovable old pair of senior citizens who want their salesperson to help them relocate are not sure where they want to be, what they want to buy, or how much they want to pay. Besides that, they have all the time in the world to decide. Is it any wonder that some experienced real estate salespeople refer to this kind of client as "missionary work"?

We mustn't fail to mention one other common problem. It is not unusual to find that a couple who were pretty much on the same track in establishing their family and raising their kids, often discover they have different goals in mind for leisure years. A man might have always dreamed of a rustic cabin in the mountains, while his wife is envisioning a luxurious condo on the beach.

One couple we know retired in New England. The wife wanted to move to warm winters, while the husband still loved the northeastern environment. They traveled back and forth, spending winters in Florida where real estate agents showed them many properties that she would have bought. Nothing suited him. By summer they were back in New England where the real estate people showed them properties there which he liked, but of course she wasn't convinced. This went on for two years. Heaven only knows how many salespersons developed ulcers in the process. Finally, on one trek they happened to stop for a night in a town in Virginia where they fell in love with its historic aura and bought a home in which they lived happily ever after. Yes, they bought direct from the seller, without the help of a salesperson!

Changes are always accompanied by some stress, and this is certainly true of moving one's abode, no matter when you do it or for what reason. It is not at all unusual to hear, a person who has just finished unloading their van, saying "Never again. You hear me, Edward? I NEVER WANT TO MOVE AGAIN!" If the move also entails a change in life style, the transition can be doubly stressful. It's a good idea to think about future as well as present wants and needs.

Choosing a location is critical. Moving to a new place – to a resort destination, for example – can be exciting for some people. Being able to play golf all year long or go to the beach every day may sound like Heaven. Others miss being removed from old friends, their beloved church, that reliable doctor and painless dentist, shopping in familiar stores and traveling on familiar roads – they wish they were "home". There are other reasons for relocating in those declining years: moving closer to family, or to a more healthful climate, or to an area that is more economical, etc. However, we have a feeling that those who haven't moved often during their lifetime, or who might find making new friends difficult, a trial period (renting rather than buying) is smart, or as one lady expressed it – keeping the back door open.

Still on the subject of that elderly person or couple, planning to move from their present home there are many choices. Developers and builders have discovered some interesting things about seniors, namely, that there are a lot of them, and they have money. Whether the senior is thinking of

84

house, condo, apartment or multi-family project, there are plenty of places to consider that are, if not for seniors only, at least "senior friendly". Look for the marketing slogan "for active adults". You'll find senior-friendly floor plans and senior friendly amenities.

In sorting out options, one major factor to consider is security. Not only single old ladies living alone, but all seniors are proving to be easy targets for criminals. Ask yourself – Does this seem safe? Also important, especially if considering moving to much smaller digs, is privacy. Some older folks who rarely enjoy a quiet night's sleep have probably already opted for separate bedrooms. Even if not, one finds retirement means much more "togetherness" than one had in the working years and so it pays to ask, do I have a space to be alone now and then?

We can also add gardening. Some consider it a chore and will be happy to escape yard care, but to a dedicated grower it is more than a hobby and closer to a religion. The gardener asks – Is there a good piece of dirt? Winnie was heartsick when her husband, in their retirement years, decided he wanted to sell the house and move to a high rise apartment in the city where he could be free at last of yard chores, and walk to restaurants and entertainment. The ultimate solution was a rooftop condo that had a broad outside area where he could locate big boxes of soil.

All of this is assuming people who have enough income to choose their digs. Unfortunately, the volatile economy we've lived in lately has denied this to even some of our most careful planners. In olden times, moving in with the kids was a common solution. There was lots of work to do around a household back then, so an extra pair of hands was welcome. Three-generational families are still a way of life in some cultures. We know of some cases where this arrangement has worked out just fine. Too often, though, the young people in a busy two-career life style, can't find the time and the space for Grandpa. We did hear one crusty old girl say "I'll be damned if I'll spend my last years in a basement!"

My neighbor, Clara, tried hard to make her mother-in-law happy when the old lady moved in with them, but there was no pleasing her. "Every morning she tells me she's praying the good Lord will take her that day," Clara cried. "Well," Clara added, "At this point, we're hoping too."

The developer of a senior condominium project in Hawaii was advised by marketing people that he needn't even try to woo buyers of Asian extraction because they were long accustomed to living in three-generational homes. He was amazed to find that 30% of the first fifty buyers were Asian and mostly women. He talked to one lady about her motivation. "Was it a search for independence or a remedy for loneliness?" he asked. "Look at the house across the street there," she replied. "Do you see that big vegetable garden, and do you see the old lady with the hoe, working in that garden?"

"Yes, I can see her," he replied. "Well," she went on, "what kind of idiot wants to spend her old age with a hoe!"

The latest trend in housing for seniors are the so-called CCRC's, which are springing up like mushrooms. CCRC stands for Continuing Care Retirement Community. They come in all sizes and price ranges, possibly having facilities for Independent Living, for Assisted Living, for Re-Hab, for Skilled Nursing and for Dementia. Most of them have healthy entry fees, and also, whether you're buying or renting, pretty stiff monthly fees. You probably have your own apartment but share an array of public rooms and facilities. As one financial planner put it, in choosing "Be sure to apply the TANSTAFL principle." (That stands for "There Ain't No Such Thing As Free Lunch.") In other words, don't expect the Ritz for the price of the YWCA.

I was a healthy, 84-year-old widow, living alone in a fairly spacious condo, when I decided to move into a CCRC. I had to adjust to a much smaller living area and a long list of rules that go with multi-family living. On the other hand I have security, delicious meals, a handy spa, housekeeping service and enjoy not having to dine alone. I can even call a maintenance man who hurries to my door when I carelessly stop up the disposal. Best of all, it provides scads of new and wonderfully compatible friends. I've discovered that I have a real talent for being pamperedd.

"I KNOW WE AGREED THAT YOUR MOTHER COULD MOVE IN WITH US, BUT I DIDN'T REALIZE THAT INCLUDED THE LADIES IN HER BRIDGE CLUB, TOO."

CHAPTER 9

If I Should Die
Before I Wake

No picture of old age would be complete without a word or two about the approach of the Grim Reaper. Once you get close to the ninety mark, your death is no longer a reality so far removed into the future that it can comfortably be ignored. The Lord only knows we are kept reminded by the frequent and noisy arrival of emergency vehicles when living in senior housing. How we program that awareness into our thoughts and actions is, of course a part of one's individual beliefs and personality. We venture to say, though, that in our experience the great majority of our seniors handle it very well indeed. Yes, they can even laugh about it – hence the oft-repeated joke about it not being a good time to buy green bananas.

A Catholic priest developed an inoperable cancer and at one point was told that he had only a few weeks at best to live. Since he happened to be a good friend, I asked him what his thoughts were upon hearing that prognosis. "Curiosity", he replied with a broad grin. "I am overwhelmed with curiosity." This was right in line with a quote I love from Shakespeare's Macbeth:

> "Nothing in his life
> Became him like the leaving it. He died
> As one who had been studied in his death
> To throw away the dearest thing he own'd
> As t'were a careless trifle.

Then there was Broadway producer Charles Frohman, who was standing on the deck of the sinking ship, Lusitania when he said to fellow passengers: "Why fear death? Death is only a beautiful adventure."

Certainly, for the truly faithful, a strong conviction in the existence of the "hereafter", and the fact that one's death will bring about a reunion with lost loved ones can be enormously helpful. That, of course , presumes one is not overburdened with sin! Do we really need to know what it will be like, and how it will happen? Probably not. On the other hand, even those who have their doubts about what death might bring do seem to greet the prospect with serenity as the last act progresses. Perhaps this represents the philosophy of the poet, Wordsworth as shown in his "Intimations of Immortality". In effect he is saying that newborn babies come to us "trailing clouds of glory", directly from God. As life progresses we stray further and further away until old age, when we find ourselves on a return path.

When my dear mother-in-law was ninety-six she was obsessed – not with dying, but with the fear that, if she died in Colorado where she was living, she wouldn't be buried in Wisconsin where her beloved husband was at rest. A helpful son-in-law told her not to worry. He'd buy her a bus ticket to Milwaukee and sit her up in a seat nice and straight. No, that didn't help. But what did was putting her on the phone with a funeral director in Wisconsin. She made and paid for all the arrangements right down to the hymns to be sung at the service. With that done, she passed away peacefully. Being prepared, so to speak, seems to make it manageable. She happened to die in Colorado on Christmas Eve. The holiday plus snowstorms across the nation made air travel a winter nightmare, but our family owed that dear lady big time, and we did manage to get her and ourselves to Wisconsin as per her wish.

Heaven knows we elderly get plenty of opportunities to attend funerals for departed relatives and friends. As one older man put it "I've lost so many good buddies lately that if pall bearing was an Olympic sport, I could make the 1st team." Fortunately there seems to be a trend to holding services on a more upbeat tone. The old style of eliciting so many tears that the audience was in danger of dehydration is rarely seen any more.

Sometimes even the passing of an old buddy like Herbert can have its humorous aspects. In his dotage, Herbert lost some inhibitions. Formerly never one to misbehave, he became a bit overly amorous. Lucy became his lady friend. One day she came to the nurse's station and said that Herbert was in her apartment, and he wasn't feeling well. The nurse came to see, and found that Herbert was lying in Lucy's bed, stone cold dead. One was left to guess what kind of exertion might have led to his demise.

Seniors may also have some experience in visiting friends and loved ones in nursing home environments. These are not so likely to be happy experiences. For some unfortunate people, dying is a long-drawn-out process. The gradual loss of physical and mental capacities, diminishing any enjoyable quality of life can be terribly depressing for anyone and also hard on those who are closest. The angel of Death seems to be hovering close by, but elusive. Loved ones can't decide whether to pray it stays away or that it might come soon. Workers who provide loving care for nursing home patients surely must be earning rewards in Heaven. It's no wonder that they sometimes call pneumonia, which is often the cause of death for long-term patients "an old man's blessing."

So, what kind of plans should we make for the last phase of our lives? Most lawyers would agree that estate planning should probably happen long before old age. You are never too young to die, and even if your worth is somewhere between poor and pitiful, each little bit of treasure should go to your chosen heirs. We knew a young couple in their thirties who had three children, and who were both killed in a plane crash. They left no will but the children received a $300,000 insurance settlement. The mother's sister and the father's brother both claimed custody, and their legal battle was waged in the courts for five years with legal fees escalating, while the children remained in foster care. Finally the court awarded the custody to the town banker, who was a distant cousin. We hasten to assure anxious readers with the fact that this type of situation is very unusual, but parents do die together in accidents in this day and age. Those who have even one baby should provide for who would be responsible in that event.

A lady we knew who was suffering from leukemia, had an estate which consisted primarily of some valuable jewelry she had inherited. She had no children but she did have five nieces. When she passed away it was discovered that she had placed each individual item of jewelry into an envelope with instructions about who should receive that piece. Three of the five would-be heirs were by-passed in favor of more distant connections. Her executor, who knew the nieces and who was confidently expecting that there might be major warfare over the jewelry, was understandably elated to find the envelopes!

Equally joyful, we feel sure, are medical personnel when they have a patient who has taken the trouble to sign "living will" and other legal steps to ensure that their wishes regarding sustaining life artificially. In the absence of any firm evidence of the patient's own wishes, this can and often does lead to very bitter family fights and even long drawn-out legal proceedings, while the patient stays in a vegetative state and costs multiply. A doctor recently told me that, even when a patient does have a living will, it is difficult to "pull the plugs", when any family member objects.

Then there is the matter of what kind of funeral services you would prefer. Personally, I tend to feel pretty much the way comedian Bob Hope did when his son asked him, on his death bed, how he wanted his tombstone inscribed. He replied, "Surprise me." We must agree, though, that once plans have been made there is a sense of satisfaction. When one lady finished making elaborate plans for her services, she was so pleased with her work that she announced that she could hardly wait.

My plan has now been made, the kids have been informed, and told that I will haunt them if they fail to carry out the program correctly. I know my family intend to treat funerals with respect and reverence, but somehow, screw-ups always seem to occur. It may go back to Mom's story of an old country service where the pall bearers dropped the coffin, which broke open and the deceased rolled down a nearby hill.

When my good friend , Peggy died, she had left me a letter with detailed instructions for her memorial services. She chose the place, the time of day, the readings, and who was to read them, the hymns and who was to sing them, and even the single American Beauty rose to be placed on the altar. Peggy was always a superb hostess, and this service was especially meaningful to those of us who loved her because it was so eminently a Peggy affair. It was almost as if she was there to greet us.

Failing to plan ahead was disastrous when Uncle Jim died suddenly in Las Vegas. His remains were cremated. An urn containing his ashes was to be placed at the front of the chapel for the services, but his urn wasn't ready yet on short notice, and a substitute was offered so that a delay wouldn't cause guests who had to travel to change plans. No one noticed the inscription on the substitute urn until the end of the service. The pastor, on exiting, called back "Be sure you all pray for Bubba, too."

Well, this topic might logically conclude with the young doctor who told an elderly lady that she should go to a "sleep clinic". When she asked why, he said "You don't sleep well. You probably have spells of apnea, and you could even die in your sleep.". "Oh, good," she replied. "That's my plan."

"I KNOW THEY'RE TRYING TO HAVE UNCLE LUTHER LOOK NATURAL, BUT I WANTED HIM HOLDING A PRAYER BOOK, NOT A DRY MARTINI."

CHAPTER 10

The Cast of Characters...

Hopefully, all of these anecdotes and scholarly insights have convinced our readers that growing old not only beats the heck out of the only alternative, but can be approached with something far short of abject horror.

Maybe it isn't the most entertaining and enjoyable phase of your life, but many people do play that last act with grace and talent. Yes, we are "set in our ways" but young people who take the time to get to know us may be surprised to find it well worth the effort.

A grandson recently asked me if I thought there was a communications "disconnect" between his generation and mine. After thinking about it, I replied that I didn't think that word was quite right. "It's more like we still live in the same solar system but on different planets," was my reply. Changes in the world around us seem to be occurring at a dizzying rate; and in the process, values and principles my generation cherished have all but disappeared. To a great extent, who we are is influenced by the world in which we grew up. I don't feel comfortable in my grandchildren's world, but then I doubt if my grandmother would have felt o.k. in mine. (She crammed her body whalebone corsets and churned her own butter.)

Who are we old people? Our childhood was spent in the deepest and longest lasting economic depression the country has ever seen, before or since. This formed habits that never left us, We still hate to see the waste of uneaten food left on a plate, and can't resist pocketing sugar packets when eating out in a restaurant.

We came of age just in time for the only war this country has ever had which posed an immediate threat to our shores and our very way of life. We still stand at attention when our national anthem is played, recite the "pledge of allegiance", and salute the flag with feeling. We won our war. It is hard to contend that that's true of any of the following skirmishes.

During our great war, millions of American women left their kitchens to board buses and take over essential jobs that were left vacant when the men went overseas. It was all part of the war effort. Needless to say, we didn't necessarily run back to our kitchens when the war ended. Once released from domestic drudgery, a lot of women had discovered a whole new way of life. They became pretty passionate about "equal rights"! The degree to which that battle changed the future may represent our generation's most significant contribution to history, for better or for worse. It has to be at least on a par with our many notable inventions which include... yes, this was one of ours... the computer. (Personally, I feel apologetic about the computer since mine definitely harbors evil spirits.) We cherish our right to vote and rarely fail to exercise it. You may have noticed that politicians are extremely careful with issues like Social Security.

The lean years imbued us with a healthy respect for money and a strong work ethic We were loyal employees, taking our jobs and careers very seriously. It wouldn't have occurred to us to begin a job interview with questions about "benefits". This particular generation of young people is coming of age, however, at a time when politics is considered to be a dirty business, and political campaigns are mud-throwing contests. The world of business ethics is as bad or worse. No wonder the "millennial" generation do not consider employment to be a #1 priority, and are not noted for company loyalty. They are setting new records in the brevity of time spent in a job before leaving for something else. We dare say that becoming jobless and therefore moneyless, might alter that attitude. Recently I told a grandson of mine that I thought he could do well in politics. "Gram, do you think I've lost my integrity?" he responded.

We were raised in a world where manners, morals and modesty ruled. These principles were well ingrained in our character by parents, who demanded and received our respect. Unacceptable behavior was handled immediately and decisively. We didn't answer questions with a yes or no. It was "Yes Sir" or "No, Ma'am". We didn't chime in on adult conversations. "Children", they used to say, "should be seen and not heard." Older people were Mr. Jones or Mrs. Smith except for a relative who could be Aunt Agatha, or a close friend who might be Miss Julia, but never by just a first name. The rules laid down by a lady named Emily Post were second only to the ten commandments.

Today, parental discipline seems to start and end with a two-minute "time out". Anything more decisive might possibly do immortal harm to our children's self esteem. A spanking now rates as 'child cruelty'. I was cruel, believing, as I still do, that the best way to stop unacceptable behavior is to lower the boom the very first time it occurs. It was not unusual to hear one of our older offspring saying to a younger one: "You better not do that, or you're gonna get it." By some miracle my seven emerged with their self esteem very much intact.

If an inconsiderate driver did some trick that annoyed my mother, she might mutter "jackass" under her breath. That was as close as she ever got to a cuss word. If we accidentally bleated out a heartfelt "damn" we might have gotten our mouth washed out with soap. Our mothers never had to search the dial for family-friendly entertainment. There was no other kind. We were not exposed to the violence and smut that is rampant on the media today. If my mother had lived to see a Cialis commercial on TV she would probably have fainted dead away.

Going out anywhere always meant dressing up. We not only dressed up for church but had to wear a hat or head covering. Even for travel we dressed up. Mother had a thing about ladies never being without clean white gloves! I feel sure she would have had a major heart attack if she had lived to see the girls on the beach in bikinis! "You aren't going out the door in that," was often heard. I still believe that what you wear has a lot to do with how you act. If you don't believe that, think about how a man changes the minute he dons a uniform. Young girls today seem to prefer clothes that leave absolutely nothing to the imagination. They won't believe this, but many men agree that a Hawaiian muumuu, which covers not only skin but also the shape, is sexier.

This is not to say that our ways were the right ways, and that this younger generation is going astray. Were we repressed? Certainly, and you can imagine that there were times when some of us felt pretty rebellious about all of those strict rules, and undoubtedly broke a few. Oddly enough, though, we don't feel we were "abused" or that our self respect has suffered. In retrospect, as we see our grandchildren being raised in a society that has become very open, casual and totally permissive, forgive us if we tend to think that a little repression wouldn't have been all bad. The idea of today's teens and even pre-teens learning to cope with sex and its consequences in middle school and high school blows my mind. I'm grateful to the good Lord that a game of spin-the-bottle was about as exciting as anything I experienced in my puberty.

How then can we crotchety old souls who must at times feel like misfits in today's society manage to grow old happily and gracefully in today's world? Observing people who are doing just that provides a few common denominators, and gives some clues to enterprising young people who might dare to try communicating with us on our wave length.

1. <u>We are positive thinkers</u>. Life is a constant parade of choices, and you can program that wondrous thinking machine on top of your neck in the process. Why dwell on past losses, missed opportunities, stupid mistakes and ancient grievances when you can <u>choose</u> to enjoy today and expect tomorrow to be even better?

2. <u>We like ourselves</u>. Considering how much time we spend with ourselves, it would be a shame to grow old without discovering that we truly do have some good qualities.

3. <u>We like to feel needed</u>. There are so many and so varied an array of needs in this world, that no one should ever have to feel that their life is without purpose. Reading to a nursing home patient, caring for a beloved pet, listening to a boring old man tell an interminable story – the list is endless.

4. <u>We try to stay busy,</u> Time is too precious a commodity to be wasted. When it comes to filling our days with activities that are satisfying and/or enjoyable, we plan accordingly rather than always depending on others. We try always to have something on the calendar that can be anticipated with pleasure. Unexpected treats and visits are nice, but better still are the ones that are planned ahead.

5. <u>We have faith</u> – of one sort or another – something to turn to when our own limitations surface, as they surely will. When we find our selves grieving for loved ones lost, as we often do, faith is the source of comfort and strength. It is the answer for questions without answers. As one old saying goes: "There are no atheists in foxholes."

6. <u>We laugh a lot.</u> Laughter is the greatest therapy for whatever-ails- you. I doubt if there is any bad day that will not be immediately improved when you can have a good old belly laugh. There are even medical specialists who will testify to the therapeutic value of watching an old Laurel and Hardy movie, or the tape of an old "I Love Lucy" or Jack Benny show.

I can't recall the title or author of a book I read years ago, about an artist who had led a very dissolute life. What I still do remember is that in the final chapter, when he is in a hospital, dying, a nun comes into his room and finds him laughing.

"You shouldn't laugh," she said. "You should be praying."

"It's the same thing, Sister," he replies. "It's the same thing."

"DON'T WORRY, GRANDMA. YOU LOOK FINE.
I DIDN'T EXPECT THAT YOU'D BE
UP ON THE LATEST FASHIONS."